Fairness

Julie Murray

Abdo
CHARACTER EDUCATION
Kids

abdopublishing.com

Published by Abdo Kids, a division of ABDO, PO Box 398166, Minneapolis, Minnesota 55439.
Copyright © 2018 by Abdo Consulting Group, Inc. International copyrights reserved in all countries.
No part of this book may be reproduced in any form without written permission from the publisher.

Printed in the United States of America, North Mankato, Minnesota.

052017

092017

THIS BOOK CONTAINS
RECYCLED MATERIALS

Photo Credits: iStock, Shutterstock

Production Contributors: Teddy Borth, Jennie Forsberg, Grace Hansen

Design Contributors: Christina Doffing, Candice Keimig, Dorothy Toth

Publisher's Cataloging in Publication Data

Names: Murray, Julie, 1969-, author.

Title: Fairness / by Julie Murray.

Description: Minneapolis, Minnesota : Abdo Kids, 2018 | Series: Character
    education | Includes bibliographical references and index.

Identifiers: LCCN 2016962341 | ISBN 9781532100086 (lib. bdg.) |
    ISBN 9781532100772 (ebook) | ISBN 9781532101328 (Read-to-me ebook)

Subjects: LCSH: Fairness--Juvenile literature. | Fairness in children--Juvenile
    literature. | Children--Conduct of life--Juvenile literature. | Social skills in
    children--Juvenile literature.

Classification: DDC 179/.9--dc23

LC record available at http://lccn.loc.gov/2016962341

Table of Contents

Fairness

Fairness is all around.

Do you see it?

Jack wants to play a game. He waits his turn. He is being fair.

Sam shares his toy with Kyla.

He is being fair.

Tess **includes** her partner.

She is being fair.

Greg plays chess with his friend. He follows the rules. He is being fair.

The lunch table is full. Kim makes room for Mary. She is being fair.

Nico **reports** to his class. The class listens. They are being fair.

Sight words

live out people
who work

4. time
5. white
6. bike
7. dime
8. hide
9. ice
10. kite

17

Gabe broke his bank. He tells the truth. He is being fair.

Were you fair today?

More Ways to Be Fair

listen to others

play by the rules

share your toys

take turns

Glossary

include
let someone share in an activity.

report
give information on a topic.

Index

abdokids.com

Use this code to log on to abdokids.com and access crafts, games, videos, and more!

Abdo Kids Code:
CFK0086